VOLUNTEERING FOR THE
ELDERLY

by Lynn Ternus

BrightPoint Press

San Diego, CA

BrightP◇int Press

© 2022 BrightPoint Press
an imprint of ReferencePoint Press, Inc.
Printed in the United States

For more information, contact:
BrightPoint Press
PO Box 27779
San Diego, CA 92198
www.BrightPointPress.com

LIBRARY OF CONGRESS CATALOGING-IN-PUBLICATION DATA

Names: Ternus, Lynn, author.
Title: Volunteering for the elderly / by Lynn Ternus.
Description: San Diego, CA : BrightPoint Press, [2022] | Series: Get involved | Includes
    bibliographical references and index. | Audience: Grades 7-9
Identifiers: LCCN 2021007413 (print) | LCCN 2021007414 (eBook) | ISBN 9781678201289
    (hardcover) | ISBN 9781678201296 (eBook)
Subjects: LCSH: Older people--Services for--Juvenile literature. | Teenage volunteers in
    social service--Juvenile literature. | Young volunteers--Juvenile literature. | Voluntarism--
    Juvenile literature.
Classification: LCC HV1451 .T43 2022 (print) | LCC HV1451 (eBook) |
    DDC 362.6/75370835--dc23
LC record available at https://lccn.loc.gov/2021007413
LC eBook record available at https://lccn.loc.gov/2021007414

CONTENTS

AT A GLANCE

- Volunteers can help the elderly in many ways. They can assist their elderly neighbors. They can visit nursing homes and assisted living facilities. They can volunteer to work in hospice care.

- Many seniors want to continue living in their homes. Help from volunteers can make that happen.

- People can help elderly neighbors with yard work. They can also volunteer to do household tasks. These things many help elderly adults better manage their homes.

- The United States has more than 15,000 nursing homes. They help about 1.3 million people. There are more than 28,000 assisted living communities in the United States. These help about 811,000 elderly adults.

- To volunteer at an elder care facility, people typically fill out an application. They may have an interview with the facility's staff. Potential volunteers may also have to go through background checks.

- Volunteers at nursing homes and assisted living facilities do many of the same tasks. They spend time with the elderly living there. They plan games and activities. They try to brighten people's days.

- Hospice care volunteers help patients live the last days of their lives in comfort. They give emotional support to both patients and families.

VISITING THE ELDERLY

Paul grabbed a bag from the trunk of his car. It was filled with art supplies. He walked toward the assisted living facility where he volunteered. It was winter, and Paul's breath came out in white puffs. The parking lot and sidewalks were scraped clean of all ice. Paul was glad. He didn't want any of his elderly friends to accidentally slip and fall.

Elderly people may struggle emotionally as they lose independence. Volunteers can help improve their days.

Paul walked into the lobby. The

receptionist behind the desk recognized

him and smiled. She told Paul he could

go into the dining room. Lunch was over.

Engaging with crafts can bring joy to an assisted living facility.

The room was clean and empty. Paul started taking the art supplies out of his bag. He took out glue, clothespins, paint, and string. He also laid out scissors, tiny sticks, and white, black, and orange felt. Today he was going to help people at the facility make snowman ornaments.

Groups of people started coming into the room. Some people walked with canes or rolled in with wheelchairs. Paul smiled and greeted them. He hugged a few of his friends who liked that kind of contact. Everyone was excited to be together.

Paul showed them how to do the art project. Sometimes he had to raise his voice a bit so people could hear him. Then Paul walked around the room. He helped anyone who needed it. Sometimes he helped people cut up felt for their snowmen. Paul also took time to ask people how they were doing. Some people in the assisted living facility were lonely. They didn't get many visitors. They were especially glad Paul was there. He brightened up their days.

HELPING SENIORS

Elderly people are sometimes called seniors. Seniors are typically defined as adults in their sixties or older. Sometimes seniors need help. They can't do all the activities and chores they used to do when they were younger. This can sometimes make living in their own homes difficult. When it becomes too hard, some older adults may move to places that give them extra help. Some go to assisted living

Elderly people may have health conditions that make doing certain tasks difficult.

facilities. These places help the elderly with

daily chores, such as cleaning. But people

in assisted living can mostly take care of

themselves. Nursing homes are a little

different. Elderly adults who need more help live there. They might need help getting to the bathroom or getting dressed. Nursing homes also give residents more medical attention.

Volunteers who work with the elderly don't need to be trained medical professionals. They find ways to make elderly adults' lives happier. Volunteers plan games and activities. They help elderly people with everyday tasks. Volunteering can take place at a person's private home, in an assisted living facility, in a nursing home, and in hospice care. Volunteering

Simply spending time with an elderly person can be important work.

with the elderly is a rewarding experience

for many people.

CHAPTER ONE

HOW CAN I HELP MY ELDERLY NEIGHBORS?

Sometimes seniors can't move around as much as they could in their younger years. This can make it hard for them to do certain tasks. People who have elderly neighbors don't necessarily need to sign up to volunteer. Instead, they can ask if their neighbors would like any help. When people

Volunteers can help elderly people stay in their own homes longer.

volunteer on their own, there is no official

supervisor watching them. They are in

charge of their own schedules. However,

people who volunteer to help elderly

neighbors need to pay attention to how their

neighbors are feeling. It's important that volunteers don't become intrusive.

HELPING WITH EVERYDAY TASKS

There are many ways to help elderly neighbors. People can do yard work. They can pick up sticks, mow lawns, trim bushes, or plant flowers. They can also help inside the home. People can vacuum. They can do laundry or take on other housekeeping tasks. In addition, houses need maintenance. Sometimes things break and need to be fixed. If a volunteer has the knowledge and experience, he or she can help fix certain things. This may be as

People can help their elderly neighbors with household cleaning.

straightforward as replacing batteries in a

smoke detector. Or it could be changing a

light bulb in a ceiling fan.

For an able-bodied volunteer, getting

on a safe and secure ladder or step stool

to replace batteries or light bulbs may not

be difficult. But for an elderly person, it

could be hard and dangerous. As people

age, they can develop risk factors that

make them more likely to fall. Some of

these risk factors are issues with balance.

Others are muscle weakness and foot

HELPING FROM ANYWHERE

People don't necessarily need to have elderly neighbors to help out seniors. At stores, people can offer to return an elderly person's shopping cart. They can retrieve items on bottom or top shelves for elderly shoppers. They can open and hold doors for seniors. If there's a long line in a store, coffee shop, or anywhere else, a person can offer an elderly adult his or her place in line. A person can also give up a seat on a busy bus or in a waiting room.

problems. Elderly adults are also more likely to get seriously hurt from falls. Volunteers might be able to help with tasks that would be dangerous for seniors. However, young volunteers should ask a parent or guardian for help with certain jobs. The adult can make sure tasks are done safely and correctly.

Volunteers can also help the elderly by running errands. Some seniors can't drive. Or they might have trouble leaving their homes. People can volunteer to go grocery shopping. That way their elderly neighbors

People can volunteer to get groceries for elderly neighbors.

don't have to walk through busy shopping

aisles or stand in long lines.

Another way to help is by offering rides.

A volunteer can drive a neighbor to a

doctor's appointment or religious service.

Volunteers can also bring a neighbor out to run his or her errands.

People can offer to help care for an elderly neighbor's pet too. An elderly adult may have a dog. But it may be difficult for him or her to walk the dog. A volunteer can offer to walk the animal. If an elderly adult has a cat, a person can clean out the cat's litter box.

Certain types of weather can be challenging for seniors. If a winter storm or hurricane is coming, volunteers can check in with their neighbors. They can see if the seniors need anything before the storm

Shoveling an elderly person's driveway and sidewalk can help keep him or her safe.

hits. Snow and ice can cause people to slip

and fall. Seniors can get seriously injured.

Volunteers can shovel a neighbor's sidewalk

and driveway. They can put salt down on

these areas to melt ice.

VOLUNTEER ORGANIZATIONS

People can join organizations to help elderly people living at home. Some communities have groups called "villages." For instance, a group called Capitol Hill Village is in Washington, DC. Elderly people sign up to be members of the village. Then volunteers and a small staff help the members with various tasks. "Such support can have a huge impact," said Jennifer Ludden, a writer for NPR. "Members say it can make the difference between feeling the need to move into assisted living and having the confidence to stick it out on one's own for a few more months—or even years."[1] There are other similar volunteer organizations. For example, Help at Your Door is based in the Minneapolis and Saint Paul, Minnesota, area. It has hundreds of volunteers.

Meals on Wheels is another popular volunteer organization. More than 5,000 communities in the United States have a Meals on Wheels program. It has more than 2 million volunteers and staff members. It helps more than 2.4 million adults ages sixty and up. Meals on Wheels volunteers deliver meals to seniors. They also visit with seniors. They perform safety

SENIORS AND YOUNG PEOPLE IN THE UNITED STATES

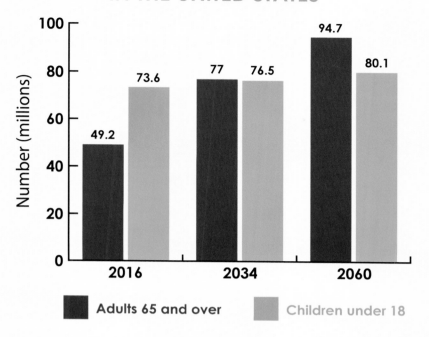

Source: "An Aging Nation: Projected Number of Children and Older Adults," US Census Bureau, March 13, 2018. www.census.gov.

People in the United States are having fewer children than people did in the 1950s and 1960s. In addition, people in the United States have a high life expectancy at seventy-eight years. Because of these two things, experts think that by 2034 there will be more seniors than children. This has never happened before in the United States.

checks to make sure people are doing

OK. Sidney is a senior who receives meals

Delivering warm, nutritious meals to elderly people helps them stay healthy.

through this program. He said that because of Meals on Wheels, he was able to continue living at home. "I feel confident of staying here. That's important to me; I'm a very independent person," Sidney said.[2]

In Meals on Wheels, people can volunteer in groups. Multiple people can visit seniors at the same time. A group of friends can volunteer. Or a family can work together to help the seniors in their community.

To volunteer at an organization, people should do some research. They should see what organizations are nearby. They need to decide what kinds of work interest them. Then they can contact organizations to ask questions. They can ask how to apply.

BENEFITS OF HELPING THE ELDERLY

Volunteering with the elderly has many benefits. Volunteers have chances to make friends with elderly adults. Also, elderly people have many life experiences.

They're often happy to share their stories and knowledge with volunteers. Marissa Salvesen is a manager at a senior living center called United Methodist Homes. She noted that many elderly people

BENEFITS OF SENIOR VOLUNTEERING

Many seniors seek out volunteer opportunities themselves. Some of them tutor or teach. Others serve as **mentors** for young people. Some seniors prepare and serve food to people. They also help clean up community areas or help construct homes. There are many different volunteer opportunities for seniors. Elderly adults who volunteer are less depressed. They feel accomplished. They create meaningful connections with new people.

have lived through historic events, such as wars. She said, "Listening to their stories can provide wisdom and insight for life, offering a new perspective for your own life circumstances."[3]

In addition, volunteers can make their elderly neighbors' lives easier. A 2018 survey showed that many seniors want to continue living in their homes. Volunteers can help make that happen. The work they do might help elderly adults live in their homes longer.

CHAPTER TWO

HOW CAN I VOLUNTEER IN ASSISTED LIVING?

People in assisted living facilities typically have a fair amount of independence. Assisted living facilities help residents with daily tasks. They may also help elderly adults take medication. In some places, residents have their own rooms

People in assisted living homes may get help with cleaning.

or apartments. They share the common areas with other people. Some assisted living centers look very similar to apartment buildings. Residents may bring their own furniture for their rooms.

The National Center for Assisted Living helps people in assisted living. It says that the United States has more than 28,000 assisted living communities. These places help approximately 811,000 people. With so many assisted living facilities, people have several different options for where to volunteer.

VOLUNTEER ACTIVITIES

Assisted living volunteers can simply socialize with elderly adults. They may play card games or do puzzles. They could take walks with seniors. Some volunteers organize activities. They may do crafts or

Helping with an exercise class is one way to volunteer.

lead exercise groups. If they know how to

play an instrument, volunteers may want to

share that talent with seniors. Volunteers

may also be able to help seniors with

technology. For example, a volunteer could

show a resident how to use video chat.

Technology can help seniors connect with

family or friends who can't visit them often.

People can use their own special skills

while volunteering. Carol Dexter had a

SPIRITUAL SERVICES

Some senior living facilities offer spiritual services to residents. Spiritual leaders may come to the buildings and hold services each week. At some facilities, volunteers can play an active role too. Some of them assist residents with getting to the service, which may be held in a large room at the facility. Some places even have a chapel on-site. Volunteers might be able to perform music during the worship service. In addition, volunteers can read holy texts, such as the Bible or the Tanakh, to residents who would like that.

career as a nurse. When she retired, Dexter started volunteering at Woodbury Senior Living in Minnesota. She got to know many of the residents. Dexter was also able to use her skills as a nurse to help. "I can use my career skills as an RN [registered nurse] and manager to identify issues to pass along to my supervisor or the floor care staff, and in some cases I can solve the issue right then and there," Dexter said. She added that volunteering with the elderly was a great experience. "The real deal with this volunteer job is to help the residents . . . feel loved as individuals; and all that requires is giving love. It is easy and fun," Dexter said.[4]

MEMORY CARE

Some assisted living facilities have memory care services. Elderly adults needing this service might have different stages of **dementia**. Trained professionals help support them. Some give residents memory therapy. Others help the residents with daily tasks. Volunteers can help in different ways.

Stephanie Kanowitz's mother lived in an assisted living facility in Virginia. The facility helped elderly people who had **cognitive** troubles, such as dementia. Kanowitz started bringing her kids and their friends

to the facility to volunteer. The kids played

games with the residents. They bowled with

plastic balls and pins. They tossed balloons

to residents. They even made crafts, such

as bead bracelets. Kanowitz saw that many

STUDENT VOLUNTEERS

Students at beauty schools sometimes volunteer in assisted living facilities. They use their skills to help residents. Some students give haircuts. Others help with nail care or paint people's nails. Students at massage schools may visit these facilities too. They offer massages to residents. Students and elderly adults can make new friendships. Students are also able to use this time to train. It helps them develop their skills.

Some elderly people enjoy visits from therapy dogs. These calm, friendly dogs are well trained and help relieve stress.

of the seniors enjoyed the interactions. She also realized kids could benefit too.

VOLUNTEER BENEFITS

Studies show that when kids visit elderly adults who have dementia, they develop important skills. They develop more patience, empathy, and problem-solving abilities. Elderly adults with memory problems benefit too. Sometimes people with dementia get very agitated. They can get restless. Or they get upset when things change. But when they are around children, they can be less distressed. They can show more interest in activities.

Volunteering at an elder care facility adds to a person's job experience. Volunteering can help a person develop important skills. This can include organizing or planning events. It can also include coordinating with

Volunteers can spend time with individual people doing activities those people love.

different people. These skills may be helpful

in different types of jobs. An **administrator**

at a nursing home or assisted living facility

may agree to be a volunteer's reference.

Usually a professional job asks an applicant

for a reference. This is a person who has

worked with the applicant. A reference can

tell a hiring manager about the person. He

or she can give information on a person's

skills, work habits, and experience. This

may help the person get the job.

CHAPTER THREE

HOW CAN I VOLUNTEER AT A NURSING HOME?

Volunteers are desperately needed in some nursing homes. Blythe Andrea realized this one day while at her child's elementary school. Her daughter's classroom was throwing a Valentine's Day party. Andrea had volunteered to help out. The day of the party, Andrea noticed the

Volunteers can help people in nursing homes get outdoors.

school's office was packed with people

there to help. They were all trying to sign in

to get into the school.

Andrea thought about her visit to the nursing home where her elderly aunt lived. There were never that many volunteers there. She said, "I did not have any problem finding a parking spot for my SUV yesterday like I did just now in the grade school lot.

COVID-19 AND THE ELDERLY

Beginning in 2020, a disease called COVID-19 swept across the United States. This disease was deadliest to seniors. Many nursing homes didn't let family, friends, or volunteers visit. They didn't want residents to get sick. This was very isolating for people living in care centers. Many seniors became depressed. In September 2020, the US government told nursing homes they should let visitors come in if the facilities didn't have any COVID-19 outbreaks.

I also did not have to wait in line at the nursing home to sign in as a visitor." Andrea wondered, "What if a quarter of the people volunteering at my daughter's grade school instead volunteered at the nursing home?"[5]

WHAT IS A NURSING HOME?

The Centers for Disease Control and Prevention is a US government agency. It notes that there are more than 15,000 nursing homes in the United States. These places help about 1.3 million people. Some people go to nursing homes for short periods of time after getting out of the hospital. That's because they still need medical care after an illness or surgery. But most people live in nursing homes full-time.

Many of these places have nurses and nursing aides available every hour of the day. They provide medical care. Some of these facilities look like hospitals. Other nursing homes are designed to make people feel more at home. Some facilities have special care sections to help people with memory issues, such as dementia. In nursing homes, elderly adults get many different care options. They have medical staff looking after them. Residents are taken care of twenty-four hours a day. They get

Elderly people, including those in nursing homes, may need help with technology.

help with everyday tasks. People may also

get speech, physical, and **occupational**

therapy from trained professionals.

Volunteers can play board games with nursing home residents.

VOLUNTEER WORK

Many of the activities volunteers do at assisted living facilities can be done at nursing homes too. Some volunteers simply spend time with the elderly people living there. They chat and play games.

These activities don't require any training. But they do require volunteers who like spending time with elderly adults.

Some facilities might have certain rules for volunteers. These rules may involve safety guidelines, professional boundaries, and patient confidentiality. Facilities may ask volunteers to follow simple rules. This can include following hygiene rules to help stop the spread of germs. For example, volunteers may be asked to carefully wash their hands before and after seeing a resident. Nursing homes may also ask volunteers to voice any concerns about an elderly person's health or conditions at the facility.

Elderly adults aren't always happy living in nursing homes. Many people miss living in their former homes. Some nursing homes aren't very cheerful places. The staff can be overworked. Residents may have to wait a while to get help from staff. Volunteers can make a big difference in making nursing homes better places to live.

Volunteers can organize dances. They can host bingo nights. They can bring cards and other games to play with people. Volunteers can get creative.

People with special skills, such as artists, can lead classes.

They should also ask residents if there is anything specific they'd like to do. That way volunteers can make sure the activities they're planning are a good fit for the residents. Writer Cordelia Hamilton noted, "Activities run by volunteers are an integral part of bringing the feeling of home to the nursing home."[6]

Volunteers can become an important part of a nursing home's community. They might become good friends with residents. They can meet a lot of different people. Talking with new people can give volunteers different perspectives on life. Volunteering helps elderly people too. Sometimes elderly adults are lonely. Their families may live far away. Or their families might not have a lot of time to visit them. This can make them feel depressed or anxious. Volunteers can improve elderly people's mental health just

Playing familiar music live at a nursing home can help bring people in the facility together.

by spending time with them. This quality

time may make elderly adults feel happy

and valued. It might also improve their

physical health. Studies show that when

elderly people feel lonely, they're at a higher

risk for heart problems. They're also at

a higher risk for strokes and dementia.

Volunteers can help elderly people feel

less lonely.

GETTING INVOLVED

Volunteer opportunities at nursing homes

and assisted living facilities are similar. So

is the process for getting involved. Every

facility is run a little differently. For instance,

some might want only people who are of

high-school age or older. If people want to

volunteer, they should do some research

first. They can talk to an administrator at the

care center. It's important to ask what kind

of volunteer opportunities the center has.

That way people can decide if the work is

something they are interested in. Then they

can fill out an application to volunteer.

ANIMALS IN NURSING HOMES

Some nursing homes allow animals to visit residents. They may even let residents have pets. Some animals seen in nursing homes are dogs, cats, birds, and fish. Seeing animals and having pets provides a lot of benefits to people. Studies show that animals can help reduce people's depression and anxiety. They can also lower people's blood pressure. Seeing animals can make residents in nursing homes feel less lonely and bring smiles to their faces.

Next, an administrator at the center

may want to meet with the applicant

face-to-face. He or she may want to make

sure the person has the right attitude to

work at the facility. Volunteers should have

great people skills. Being helpful and patient

is also important. Sometimes elderly adults

need a little extra time or help with tasks.

Volunteers need to show kindness and

compassion to the people they work with.

Some facilities want applicants to

go through background checks. These

checks let the places know if an applicant

has a criminal record. They may not want

Many great friendships can form while volunteering for the elderly.

someone who committed certain crimes

working at their facility. Both nursing homes

and assisted living facilities need to make

sure the people living there are safe.

CHAPTER FOUR

HOW CAN I VOLUNTEER IN HOSPICE CARE?

Hospice is also known as end-of-life care. It's a path people may choose when they have a terminal illness. They may not want to go through difficult medical treatments anymore, even if these treatments may help extend their lives. In other cases, their doctors realize the

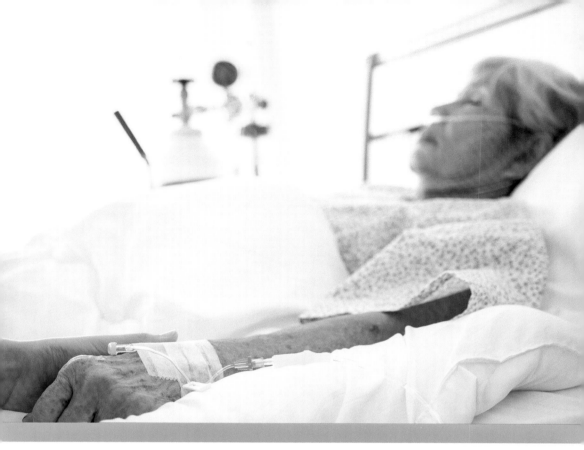

The goal of hospice is to make people's last days as comfortable as possible.

treatments aren't working. Hospice care

helps patients live comfortably for the rest

of their lives. Typically doctors recommend

hospice care to people who have fewer

than six months to live.

Hospice care is given to people living at home, in assisted living, in nursing homes, and in hospitals. People who choose hospice care get a team of people to help them manage the last few months of their lives. The team includes

SPECIFICS OF HOSPICE CARE

Members of the hospice care team work to control the patient's symptoms. They also help the person manage any pain. The team offers support for a person's mental health and helps him or her manage stress. In addition, the team works to give a patient any spiritual support he or she wants. There are approximately 4,300 hospice organizations in the United States. They help about 1.4 million people every year.

nurses and doctors. It can also include spiritual counselors and social workers. In addition, trained volunteers can make a big difference in a person's quality of life while in hospice care.

Arlene Carney is a hospice volunteer. She knows some people are hesitant to spend time with people who are dying. It might make them uncomfortable. But she doesn't feel that way. "I'm not there about the death; I'm there about their life," Carney said. "I'm still celebrating with them the life that they have. And because they're alive they . . . want to talk . . . and they want to laugh."[7]

WHAT DO HOSPICE VOLUNTEERS DO?

Hospice volunteers aim to make a patient comfortable. They also show a great deal of compassion. These volunteers help both the patient and the patient's family. They may make meals. Volunteers can also do small household tasks wherever a patient is living. They may run errands, such as grocery shopping, or take walks with a patient.

One of the simplest ways hospice volunteers make a difference is by just spending time with a patient. They can also do small activities with a patient, such as

Hospice volunteers may spend time with patients.

reading, playing music, or watching TV with

him or her.

Volunteers often give both patients and

their family members emotional support.

They want to make the family members'

Visiting with hospice patients can give them friendship.

lives easier. They might pick up kids from

school or babysit them. They might also

go shopping for the family. Volunteers

may even help take care of pets. Each

of these things can take pressure off

family members who might be under a lot

of stress.

In addition, volunteers can work with hospice support groups. Support groups help people deal with grief. These can be helpful to people who have lost loved ones. Volunteers assist group leaders. They may hand out refreshments to people attending the meetings.

Volunteers also help behind the scenes. They may work with hospice organizations to send newsletters and other mail to people. These things educate people in the community about hospice services. In addition, volunteers may help set up events for the hospice organization. Some events may be fundraisers. Others are more

focused on **advocacy** and education.

BECOMING A HOSPICE VOLUNTEER

People who want to volunteer in hospice

care should contact hospice groups near

them. They can ask questions about

GETTING INVOLVED IN HOSPICE CARE

Many hospice care volunteers want to start working in hospice after losing a loved one. Al Poeppel started volunteering after his mother got sick. "My mother was on hospice, and when I saw the good they did, I needed to give back," he said. But people who have lost a loved one need time to grieve. Many organizations encourage people to wait a bit before volunteering.

"Become a Volunteer," Hospice Foundation of America, *n.d. https://hospicefoundation.org.*

the organizations. They can figure out if their skills are a good match. After finding an organization that is a good fit, a potential volunteer can fill out an application. The application may ask how often a person is available to volunteer. It may also ask if a person is interested in working directly with a patient or if he or she would rather do behind-the-scenes work. Some hospice groups have age requirements for volunteers. In addition, hospice organizations often want to run background checks.

Volunteers who want to bring a therapy animal will need additional training.

Hospice volunteers need training. Different organizations may have different types of training. The Hospice Volunteer Association (HVA) notes that the training can be twenty to thirty hours long. It takes a few weeks to complete. Volunteers learn about hospice. They will also hear about emergency procedures in case they need to help a patient. Volunteers learn important communication skills. These are necessary to help support and comfort people. HVA notes that volunteers spend an average of four hours working each week. Many hospice organizations ask volunteers to commit to one year of work.

BENEFITS

Many hospice volunteers feel good about their work. They know they're providing an important service. However, this type of volunteering can also be hard. For some volunteers, it's difficult to know that the person they're with doesn't have a lot of time left. It can also be upsetting when the person eventually passes away. But the work has many benefits. It can give people new perspectives on life. They may not be bothered as much by small, everyday annoyances. Some people say the work makes them grateful for what they have. It also gives them a sense of purpose.

Kathy Tenuta is a volunteer at Hospice Alliance. It is a nonprofit hospice organization. She's been there for thirteen years. Tenuta said, "My journey in

Volunteering for hospice care can give people a new perspective about situations they may encounter in their own lives.

volunteering . . . has taught me that every

day is a gift, even our final ones. I believe

we bring sunshine to the darkest days. . . .

I try to do this by treating each and every one of our patients as if they were my own family." Tenuta added:

This is a passion and a purpose of mine. I have made so many wonderful "hospice" friends over the years. Some friendships are for a very short period of time, some longer, but they all leave their footprints in my heart.[8]

MAKING A DIFFERENCE

People can volunteer for the elderly in their own neighborhoods. They can help out in nursing homes or assisted living facilities. Volunteers are also needed in hospice

There are many ways to help the elderly.

care. No matter where people decide to volunteer, their work is important. It helps elderly adults feel less lonely. It brings smiles to people's faces. Volunteering is also a way for people to give back to their communities.

GLOSSARY

administrator

a person who is in charge of running a facility or organization

advocacy

the act of supporting a purpose or cause

cognitive

relating to a person's ability to remember, reason, or think

dementia

a condition in which a person has cognitive difficulties, such as troubles with memory, thinking skills, focus, or similar difficulties

mentors

individuals who are trusted guides and counselors for other people

occupational therapy

a personalized medical treatment that helps people who have certain limitations undertake activities needed for daily life

supervisor

a person who oversees another's activities

SOURCE NOTES

CHAPTER ONE: HOW CAN I HELP MY ELDERLY NEIGHBORS?

1. Jennifer Ludden, "'Villages' Help Neighbors Age at Home," *NPR*, August 23, 2010. www.npr.org.

2. Quoted in "Back to Stories: Sidney," *Meals on Wheels America*, 2020. www.mealsonwheelsamerica.org.

3. Marissa Salvesen, "The Benefits of Volunteering at a Senior Living Community," *United Methodist Homes*, April 8, 2014. www.umh.org.

CHAPTER TWO: HOW CAN I VOLUNTEER IN ASSISTED LIVING?

4. Carol Dexter, "My Volunteer Story," *Woodbury Senior Living*, August 8, 2018. https://woodburyseniorliving.com.

CHAPTER THREE: HOW CAN I VOLUNTEER AT A NURSING HOME?

5. Blythe Andrea, "16 Things I Learned by Volunteering at a Nursing Home," *LinkedIn*, June 4, 2018. www.linkedin.com.

6. Cordelia Hamilton, "How to Volunteer in a Nursing Home," *How Stuff Works*, n.d. https://money.howstuffworks.com.

CHAPTER FOUR: HOW CAN I VOLUNTEER IN HOSPICE CARE?

7. Quoted in "Arlene Carney: Fairview Hospice Volunteer Reflects on Her Inspiration to Support Others Nearing the End of Their Life," *Fairview Health Services*, *Facebook*, September 15, 2015. www.facebook.com.

8. Quoted in "Stories from Volunteers," *Hospice Alliance*, 2021. www.hospicealliance.org.

FOR FURTHER RESEARCH

BOOKS

Walt K. Moon, *Volunteering for the Homeless.* San Diego, CA:
BrightPoint, 2022.

Jean Rawitt, *Volunteering: Insights and Tips for Teenagers*. Lanham, MD:
Rowman & Littlefield, 2020.

INTERNET SOURCES

"Your Go-To Guide for Volunteering with Seniors," *AARP*, n.d.
https://createthegood.aarp.org.

"Volunteer to Help the Elderly," *Senior Care*, n.d. www.seniorcare.com.

WEBSITES

National Council on Aging
www.ncoa.org

The National Council on Aging helps seniors as they grow older. It
advocates for seniors and tries to improve their lives and help them
overcome struggles.

National Institute on Aging
www.nia.nih.gov

The National Institute on Aging is a US government organization. It strives
to understand aging, and it works to extend how long people can lead
healthy, active lives.

RELATED ORGANIZATIONS

Meals on Wheels America

1550 Crystal Dr., Suite 1004
Arlington, VA 22202
info@mealsonwheelsamerica.org
www.mealsonwheelsamerica.org

Meals on Wheels America is a network that helps member organizations across the United States. It supports thousands of organizations that work to end senior hunger and isolation. More than 2 million volunteers and staff bring healthy meals to seniors, check to make sure they're doing OK, and simply spend time with them. These activities help seniors live with dignity and independence.

Volunteer Match

409 13th St., Suite 800
Oakland, CA 94612
www.volunteermatch.org

Volunteer Match is a nonprofit group that helps connect people with volunteer opportunities. Since 1998 the organization has referred more than 16 million people to different volunteer organizations. Individuals interested in volunteering for the elderly can find facilities and groups near them to contact about volunteer work.

INDEX

IMAGE CREDITS

ABOUT THE AUTHOR

Lynn Ternus is a children's book editor and author. She lives in northern Minnesota and loves spending time with and learning from her elderly grandparents.